CON

JO

CONTINUOUS JOURNEY

ERIC ASHWELL

Paper Doll

First Published in 1998 by
Paper Doll
1 Hutton Close
South Church
Bishop Auckland
Durham

ISBN : 1 86248 021 4

Typeset and Printed by
Lintons Printers, County Durham.

*In gratitude for family support over the
chequered years and recently for
Helen's help in compiling*

Many poems were first published separately
in anthologies,
mostly through Forward Press,
Peterborough
but some by:
Mast Publications
The International Library of Poetry
The Poetry Guild
Penhaligon Page

CONTENTS

FROM A SMALL THING

When I feel the enveloping dark,
The outlook bleak and future choices stark,
I into the garden often go
And plant a little seed to grow.

Sometimes my health gives concern,
Fearful that it may not return;
The only action I can upliftingly do
Is to watch the grounded seed spring through.

At the times the demands drop in at the door
Printed in painful lines red raw,
I live from day to the following day's hour;
But seed may bring next year's bower.

The bubbling children home from school
Question life and death and worldly rule;
Then I take them to observe and heed
The before and after of the seed.

When the winter's cold, damp and dull,
The clouds moving wild, low and full,
To the greenhouse this time I escape
And early colour endeavour to create.

When occasionally a friend comes to stay,
Seeking relief from his hectic way;
We lounge away the sunny day
Enjoying the flowers where once the seed lay.

Kindly then my friend will ask and wonder,
How I cope at other times than in the pleasant
summer;
Honestly to him must concede, I need the earthly
creed
As declared in the cycle of the common seed.

PONDER THE DREAM

They say that the interpretation of dreams
Is the gateway to understanding
The mystery; of what puzzling seems
To be the mix of our body and being.

What then is to be made?
Of a fantasy so dramatically displayed
To me, there where, a captive I fretfully dozed;
Near to a mass grave of bones sickeningly exposed.

Two guards were talking nearby,
One so gay on that red letter day
For his birthday had come with the bright sunrise;
But all around the holocaust and awful demise.

A young woman one companion in the lost,
Lay close, a step only from the pit;
To be taken next day at the most
By those guards and flung away like waste.

Her face was gaunt, all personality drained,
The character undressed naked and bare;
Incoherent without an intelligible voice,
But still the eyes gave a sparkle of care.

Their conversation had turned them on;
Feebly but with great resolution
She picked a slender blade of grass,
And held it out to the man
Whose anniversary that day did belong.

I remember the richness of that gesture;
For a worthless present she did offer
But of all that was available to her
In that desolate and terrible scene
A reflex action of latent loving esteem.

The giving was so much a sacramental act,
An outward and visible releasing
Of an inward and welling-up feeling;
A natural compulsive love still lingering at the
                                                           last beat.

I awoke and the story was broken;
How the guard responded to the humble action
I did not see and cannot write down.
For that awaits another night's vision.

Dreams fade and memory can falter,
But when I the thin wafer and sip of wine accept,
I recall well that simple symbolic gift;
So vividly shown to me while I slept.

HOME REASSURING HOME

It had been a very harrowing day;
Nothing had gone right along the way;
What is more my weakness had been brought to
light
And I was glad to slam tight the door that night.

But through the evening I never really recovered
From the bruising I had for many hours suffered;
Even the soft and comfortable bed did not cast off
The depression lingering and thoughts sad enough.

I had fears of a tossing sleep,
Waking up defeated before I took the leap
Into the next day, maybe a little better than before;
But offset by the lack of energy held in store.

Then suddenly there was generated a warmth
Of self glow and a feeling of personal worth;
A knock at the bedroom door, a family face,
A loving 'Good night dear and God's bless and
grace'.

ACROSS THE ACADEMIC DIVIDE

He was not too clever,
But then he was not very dull;
The man who earned his living
By his hands and strength in service for another.

Not able to control his life or destiny
In any major or minor way,
His enforced philosophy - sufficient for the day;
That will be followed by that of tomorrow.

Many were the times I talked soft to him
About the wealth in literature's treasure chest;
The elevating nature of selective reading
The pleasure of enjoying other's bequest.

Many were the times with assurance I did discuss
The certainty of mathematical proof;
Of differential and integral calculus,
Of making its exactness work for us.

I conversed often also with him
About the goal of theology's aim;
Making sense out of life's random happenings,
The destiny of man's sojourn on this earthly
                                    realm.

Then of late I long held his hand
During his illness as a friend;
And watched him approach the final end,
Calm and brave into the future beyond.

'You gave so much for him to discern
Of your guiding and erudite thought;
But what did he give in return,
To balance your efforts and concern?'

'Since you use the terms of earthly commerce
I must honestly say,
I do not know how deep went my wide discourse;
But oh yes! He showed me how to die!'

ALPHA AND OMEGA

In the beginning:

God	carries out,
	man falls about.
God	directs,
	man objects.
God	proposes,
	man opposes.
God	incarnates,
	man debates.

In the end:

God	resigns,
	man declines.

REWARD

There was a man who dug a hole,
The harder he worked the more he was lost poor
soul;
He met a man from the other side
Who talked and talked though he thought he lied;
But on crossing over he found in a lift he could
ride.

CLIMATE

There was a man often under the weather,
The winter's bitter frost made him so blue,
Whilst the summer's warmth turned him much
redder;
The autumn hue a mixture of the two
But in the spring he delicately blossomed and
grew.

LAND MINES

Twenty years or more of Civil War,
Had finally come to an exhausted end;
There really was no victory, no defeat in the event,
Just a physical tiredness
With the destructive madness all spent.

The pen of peace could hardly be held,
Weary eyes half saw the document's word;
The reason for conflict in remembrance all blurred,
But sufficient the point had been made,
Though what that was could not now be declared.

Both opposing leaders claimed their rewards,
Staking their claim to the changing times;
Each said 'My peace I leave with you,
And so after the upheaval and strain
Let the white flowers grow again!'

Yes! Let the white flowers grow again,
In a ground polluted with the land mine;
Far and wide, uncharted, hidden and unseen,
A menace to the present
And future generations of descent.

Like a malignant destructive gene,
Dormant through many a reproductive round;
But every now and then declaring its lease,
Making mayhem and tragically to remind
Of a legacy that cannot be unbequeathed.

Project the scene to the mind's eye;
Of a loving child not yet born,
Wishing to give a mother flowers to arrange and
                                        show;
But she having to correct and scold with an
                                inward cry
'No! you must leave the white flowers alone to
                                grow.'

Is this the peace that was given,
The freedom that war did bestow?
A garden of Eden out of bounds,
A present from God which dare not be taken;
Where white flowers do sickeningly grow.

NOT WHAT IT SEEMS

Often truths are spoken in the Orthodox
Though at times they do not ring true;
Some other form of language is needed,
To express ideas anew.

Poetry possesses it in an inspired rhyme,
As does music with an haunting tune;
In a life's example caught not taught over passing
time,
But above all the Paradox so contrary.

Ideas akin to the insane,
Come from the Paradox sublime;
We must serve others in order to be set free,
Grow backwards to a little child again.

To die is yet to better live,
And all these seem opposite to normal sense,
Standing reality upon its head;
Reversing the meaning of what is literally said.

In truth most is not what it seems,
So new thoughts must be brought to the public
domain;
We must lose our discipline say the absurd,
Give up correctness in order to gain.

OUR GLOBE

The world compares to the rounded onion,
In geometrical contour shaped samely;
Growing still to a destined maturity,
But in danger of a distorted mutation.

The world is tiered like the layered onion,
With humankind mixed in race, creed and need;
In sub-cultures loosely bound,
Together tightly in a whole.

All share life and common sustenance,
But with little mutual understanding or care;
Near strangers on a communal land,
Bitterly seasoned and diverse.

The world is yet more like the onion,
Which when peeled in its rawness;
Brings burning tears to pitying eyes.

HOLDING FAST

The world has in this eventful century
Been on some exponential curve of discovery,
Like the $E = mc^2$ equation of relativity,
But the important question is: its controlling
$$capacity.$$

The line shoots ever upwards
To a vast undiscovered heaven beyond;
Can our collective minds fully comprehend
Knowledge that is expanding away to the spread
$$out stars?$$

Motor car and space probe,
Mass communication immediately over the globe;
Nuclear power at the irreversible press of a button,
Penicillin to help but others to greviously govern.

Will the roller coaster keep to the rails
And draw up safe at the alighting station?
Old problems are solved but new and some still
$$posed,$$
No more so than thoughts on the final destination.

We must keep a steady nerve,
By no means reverse the adventurous verve;
But forget not the things of the past
If they bear the truths that are meant to last.

A MID-WINTER DAWN

Far from the Westland that he knew,
Was the motorist on this break of day;
When out of the fading night, eastwardly,
Gradually, so frighteningly and awefully,
There loomed gaunt Dartmoor
With a sheepdog of a town at its feet.

This was no mirage of a mind,
Deranged and desperate for fantasy;
For to him it was real, shaped substantially.
Those scene changers of the natural stage,
Who work to no play no script,
Had contrived to backcloth
A long black cloud flat,
With wisps of daylight gleaming on top.

In another place, to another mentality,
The impact night have been different;
But to this routine driver it was as shock treatment,
Lifting the depresing hand of familiarity.

It continued to captivate and entrance,
Until the destined bend allowed only a last glance.

BOWING OUT

I am past the prime athletic day,
Now I must pace the slower way;
'Come with us,' the younger energetically say,
But sorry no! It is time to stay.

This doing I can extend the span
Of a life which long ago began,
By taking the role of passive man;
And being of what reduced value I can.

There will come a moment to ebb away,
Caused by another whose plan I cannot sway;
'Your going delay,' the younger will pray 'stay',
But sorry so! This time not for me to say.

METHINKS WE PROGRESS TOO MUCH

Technology has come a long way
From my far-off salad day,
When potato crisps were salted by
The contents of a hidden coloured container dry.

Development may advance the cause
By relentless progress without pause,
Of indulgence to our pampered taste buds
With instant choice and the latest fads.

But to seek out and eventually find,
Is a thrill the present age is denied;
For it was a stimulating reward indeed,
An explosion of joy, in a moment touched
By a substance blue paper wrapped.

CACTUS VALLEY

For years and years and dreary years
I travelled the cactus valley;
And when the wind blew even mildly,
The swirl affected the senses adversely.

Not being adventurous or foolhardy,
(I do not know which in all honesty)
I kept to the familiar way,
For at least in the misty heat
I could feel the well worn
Weathered path under my feet.

The scene was colourless and without lustre,
But legends told of another ground cover
With a sea of bloom, a feast of blossom
Carpeting the drab valley bottom.

Then one routine regulated day,
Drugged with depressing boredom and monotony,
I jarred against a stone (in retrospect very fortunately).
For a while my jangled body
Was a mass of disorientated parts,
Until the spasm of pain that teared my eye
Sharpened my feelings and lifted me high.

There all around a garlanded garden did lie,
For in their own time the cacti
Had come into bud and so rarely flowered;
The predicted Eden but sadly fleeting and always lost.

Life is that cactus wide ravine,
The plants the working of the spirit,
I weary and insensitive being
Nearly missing the revealing moment,
And having again demoralising again,
To wait and wait and longer wait
For another beacon's flash to lighten the desert
                                                    scene.

THE RIVER IVEL - A PORTRAIT

The grass grows tall from the bed
Of the gentle flowing river;
It bows just below the surface
And magnifies the motion of the water.

A green moving fibre is added
To the dull coloured liquid grey,
As it runs slowly and quietly away;
Yet no wind is to be noted.

Just as a weave can give a brighter sheen
To the web of a roll of cloth;
So does the subterranean growth
Liven up the aquatic mass at the scene.

Time will bring again more puritan wear,
For dredgers will come and tear away;
Leaving a deep sighing memory
As for an old favourite suit of yesterday.

INTERCITY THOUGHTS

We see the High Speed train rushing through;
Feel the slipstream of new places and adventure,
And live in the spider's web
Of our imaginings and unfulfilment.

Sometimes however the train will stop
At our wayside station and we catch the sight
Of an haunting face, a dignified posture;
Exchange maybe an uncontrollable smile,
And we have forever a precious moment
Ever receeding away.

Precious moments then shining through the mist of
                                                    time,
Nothing worth, only to those who were there;
A restricted code known only by few,
Financially valueless, not exchangeable like a share.
A still healthy mind receives
The beams of long ago, weaker but true;
The sensitive heart responds
To joy, sadness, regret, or a mixture of many more.

Some day the recalling channel will sever;
Of no consequence to an unknowing world,
Like a shooting star witnessed
By a solitary nomadic wanderer
At a particular time and then departed;
Diminishing the store of the unshared universe,
One more entry in the encyclopedia of loss.

STRUGGLE

There is only one story worth the telling,
The root of all drama;
In many plots and counter plots swelling,
The essence of the breadth of human living.

There is one important study worth the puzzling,
The source of wide deep division;
In every culture and people dwelling,
An energy distracted and very consuming.

There is a serious truth worth the knowing,
The basis of much understanding;
In all situations and conditions applying;
A vigilance trying but necessary the keeping.

It is: good and evil ever fighting,
In the heart, in the world, always conflicting.

FROM MOEL FINDEG

High above the village of Maestafn
Is a wooded path bushy laden;
But to give the climber his entitled due,
On top is a panoramic view.

There in the long distance,
On this particular fine day I instance;
Was the city of Liverpool
Bathing its feet in the Mersey water cool.

A city doubling in many a thing,
Two football teams red and blue;
Two cathedrals of different Christian hue,
But international trade singly to pursue.

Symbolised by the imposing Liver,
There overlooking the river trade counter;
Exchanging good in the world by business,
Though sometimes in the past tainted by baseness.

On this day, from the hill top station,
No spectators' roar was heard, no bells or church
                                                    choir,
No Beatle sound, no laughter from the local humour;
Everything dozing silent, renewing for the nation.

They say that Moel Findeg where I stand in time
May be blasted away and quarried for lime;
A place of loss of which to rue
And not be able to take in the estuary anew.

But city do not mourn if this should happen
To stop your just admiration;
Your glory is not only in a scene to continue
For your cosmopolitan pulse to a colourful
                                    heritage is true.

THE HOLLYHOCK

If the foxglove is the parish spire,
Then the hollyhock is the cathedral,
The Mother Church of the garden diocese.

Towering tall from the cultivated land,
It proclaims its message grand
From the fanfare of trumpets on the stem.

But what is the message given out,
From this edifice whose glory shone
Even greater in the soil of cottages bygone?

Well it swings to the gentlest of zephyr,
And captures the slightest prompting of the spirit,
An antenna for the signals from far higher.

All other flowers then take their cue,
And pay their worshipping due
To a cloudless summer heaven.

Whilst in the air, white angels, without sound,
Disguised as butterflies fly pastorally around.

MAYTIME

The evening scent of early May
Is strong upon the spray;
A fragrance that will not allow deny
As we go our preoccupied way.

The covering blossoms of flowering May
Are noticed now with clearer sight;
Even soft pastel shades give deeper display
In the diffused slow fading light.

Take stock, enjoy the gifted dowry,
Relax in the changing circle of time;
It cannot be altered or slowed to tarry,
So live with and savour the passing glory.

Memory can so far extend the beauty,
Yet the future will delight the same way;
All is looped in one rolling gyre,
But we wait the return another year's day.

THE OLD CHALICE

Many voices have responded Amen,
Many sips taken from the curved rim,
Drinking the contents therefrom.

Many lips have given the welcome kiss,
And hearts experienced homecoming bliss,
But have also felt the departing stress.

Many wines have filled the cup,
To be emptied to the very last drop,
Yet the timeless sap still rises up.

Many faiths have been declared
In the simple act expressed,
Humbly have come, likewise have left.

The hallowed chalice; the outward expression
For many grateful thanks once given,
On the restoration of a deposed living;
In a time past of deep division.

The thought was the Silversmith's to make,
To mould and to shape,
And last while others care and appreciate.

A spirit of creation was then at work
During the labour untaken,
The spark of genius in the task.

Only now brought out for special occasions,
Its venerated use has spanned the generations,
To hold, and be of itself a treasure trove.

It is kept polished and always shines,
Plated by the caress of folk of all kinds,
But with one common belief in their minds.

To take the vessel and to use,
Is a glove-like extension of my hand,
So comfortable and reassuring to dispose;
An honour and pride to be of a continuous band.

There, together, at the altar stood,
Craft and time, wine and blood,
Are in a moment all enshrined.

FAITHFUL SERVICE

O Lord not our will
But Your will be done still.

Not our own desiring
Be paramount but Your fulfilling.

Channel well the daily striving
To swell Thy Spirit's working.

So that in the end Your glory,
Not ours, be the unfolding story.

GUIDING HOPE

O Lord be my vigilant watchtower;
Alert me to the dangers from afar,
That I may prevent those who would hurt
Going beyond the staying hour.

Then will be required another grace,
To move on and enmity to replace;
For a deed once done leaves a terrible trace,
As seen in the mark on a scarred face.

THE SOLITARY EVENING PRIMROSE

The evening light slowly fades away,
At the end of a warm summer's day;
All things put on their night attire,
And to their weary dreams retire.

But one extends the daylight hour,
By lighting up her lantern tower;
Helping the friendly sight to stay,
While shadowy bats wait to play.

Everything shortly will be locked and gone,
After the evening's watering has been done;
Only then is left the prayer and care,
Of the garden's tall lady with the lamp.

She will watch through the uncertain night,
But the flame will go out when tomorrow is
                                    bright;
It will be re-kindled for the following dark,
To continue the self-effacing work.

THE ROBIN

Of all the bosses I have known
Throughout my working days,
The little Robin is I own
The one to govern me always.

He comes when I with fork or spade
Do overturn the garden bed,
He stands very close to me
On legs of cotton thread.

He whispers orders in my ear,
Stares me long eye to eye;
He lords it well over me
And takes the worms as his rightful due.

For me his yeoman's smock is the royal display,
So his toiling subject I loyally stay.

HALFWAY HOUSE

The Christmas story tells of a halfway house,
Where God came to meet human kind;
And Shepherds and wise men did in turn reciprocate,
So that thought was not the same since that date.

A later Christmas event of much less significance
Is an annual reunion of a family split by distance;
Midway between the towns of their separate residence,
Where meaningful gifts are exchanged with added
                                        loving presence.

Gossip and news are all mulled over,
Isolated lives the more filled for the next year
With links forged still stronger;
Offsetting the corrosion of time and fading memory.

How long the custom will continue so,
There at the roadside transport cafe is hard to know;
But will cease in time because of age and natural
                                        mortality,
A small thing of the past lost in the ongoing destiny.

That it is worth doing the family would all agree,
Though of little concern to the wider community;
A random happening it cannot be expected to note and
                                        see,
And of course not world disturbing in any important
                                        degree.

But who knows out of straw and silage,
Out of sausage brunch and cups of beverage,
When the story is told by relatives who come
                                    after,
Will dawn a deeper understanding of that birth so
                                    humble;
A long time ago in a Bethlehem stable.

CHANGING RELATIONSHIPS

Man cannot live by bread alone,
A truth that is wisely known,
For he is a combined mix,
In a physical and psychological complex.

But then man cannot live by himself alone,
So must relate to others of his kind;
If that relationship goes badly awry,
Pain and confusion is the stony way.

Human lives must with neighbours share,
Like a note on a musical score;
Which arranged aright inspiring harmony made,
But if wrong all is discordant and jarred.

Adam and Eve were together in the golden summer,
A glorious season so sadly lost,
That we still search to recover,
The enlightened innocence of that age before.

The scene is clearly set in our minds,
The script remembered well with wistful sighs;
But now the players have moved with time,
And role reversals are in the caster's design.

How will the change affect the changeless need?,
Is it possible that both past and present
Can mutually respect and advance every fulfilment;
But still remain within humankind's containment?

THE OTHER SIDE OF FEAR

A sick bedroom I remember I clearly remember;
A child full of feverish distemper,
Light headed from that and the doctor's prescription,
Lay there musing between each parental visitation.

A heavy wallpaper the child saw he deliriously saw;
Gay coloured and of definite pattern,
As was the style and fashion
Long ago in a lifetime's span.

As he pondered periodically, flittingly;
The strokes of a repeated design
Would take on life and mortality,
Movement and a depth's dimension.

School over for the day, the fantasy-led day;
The voices of his friends and gay
Chatter at their games and action,
Would disturb distract the mental medication.

So it was fifty wearying years on;
The man wondered if he could
Have the courage the fateful courage,
To undergo that uncertain operation.

He thought of a distracting world,
A wide window a convalescing bed,
And a time to watch the clouds roll by.

THE GOLDEN ERA OF LOVE

Gold is the medal of the Champion,
The token of the supreme gain;
Given with a most precious of metal,
Its rarity raising it above the common vein.

Gold is the material of the wedding ring,
The token of a most heartfelt promising;
Given again with a most precious of metal,
To illustrate a love rich and special.

But if the gold were more available,
Its symbolic value would decline with increased
                                    exchange
For in other ways it has a limited usage,
And would not command such wide prestige.

If however that love which it expresses,
Rare in itself as the metal refined,
Were to be had in more plenty;
It would bring added joy to our shared entity.

Gold hard to find and in earth finite,
Love an emotion, self-propagating, which could
                                    be infinite.

CRIME AND PUNISHMENT

It seems often before Easter,
There is much brooding on death and pain;
Not only because of the Christian Passion,
Though this does set the tone.

By chance or not there is account,
Some disturbing news of awesome event,
Involving capital or corporal punishment;
Our silent impotence taken as acquiese.

Prayers are for a blanketed leap in time,
When things are past as in a bad dream;
But we know still from the heavy sadness,
Our emotional stress and the lawful due process.

With sickening regret some will start the count,
By a wild or savage act;
And sorry the qualified innocent,
Caught sometimes in the inescapable net.

Society will then respond with measured
                                    relentless pace
To extract deliberate and considered price
Of an eye for an eye return of like;
The balancing of the scale by requite.

At Easter we honour a life taken on a common
                                                    stage,
But surely not the method of that age;
For all should honestly own
The resurrection was unique not of itself the pain.

Our agonising has still not gone,
Two thousand years of thought further on.

THE WIDOW'S MITE

There had been much planned for the day,
All to be looked forward to with joy;
Then the coin was lost and must be found,
Hence the tear of disappointment profound.

It wasn't inevitable that it happened this way;
Strict control was exercised day by day,
In the handling of her limited tender,
Nevertheless wounded pride was pained by the
                                    salted tear.

No reserve bank account was open to access
To cushion the monetary loss;
Society's ways helping this to be so,
Briefly causing a self-pitying weep to flow.

When effort and determination were rewarded;
With the mite back again in safe keeping,
A thankful prayer had been offered,
And an eye sparkle returned through the watering.

The simple story illustrates not the ill
Of money desire being the root of all evil;
But as the hymn also hopes to show,
There is a love that will not let you go.

ANIMAL RIGHTS

Two hedgehogs lay on the side of the road,
One curled up and supposed asleep.
Peeringly I looked and longingly hoped,
To see the slight in and out
Of breathing taking place;
But no! Tragically it was dead.

A short distance away the other.
No need here to ponder
On life or death,
For it was a squashed skin
In a pool of bristle, blood and gut;
A sickening scene, so near and yet so far
From natural home and habitat.

Why they wanted to cross the road,
We shall never nor need to know,
Animals are entitled to go their lawful ways,
But pay a price if they move
Outside man-made reservations.

If ever planetoidal pilgrim fathers land,
Go forth and multiply
On this broad and beautiful earth;
Our innocent and harmless wandering
Could become as uncertain and as dangerous
As they were to those creatures,
On this sad, sad day.

THE THREE ON THE CROSS

Blameless or to blame,
The excruciating pain was the same;
Each taking suffering in his own way,
A mental anguish hard to stay.

Together or at different pace,
Death at the end they would share;
From different birth and parental nuture,
But their finality all at one place.

Amongst the total utter darkness,
Isolated in that still living loneliness;
Theirs was the only common companionship,
Travellers three through the terrible night.

When it was all over,
No bells as for Agincourt;
Only the sentiment did linger,
Latent, waiting to be caught.

For he today that sheds his blood with me
Shall be my brother,
Be he ne'er so noble or so vile;
But sympathy to those they did touch awhile.

GREAT AND SMALL

They were going to see the astronaut;
To talk to the man,
Who had risked all on the skyward quest,
Those reporters from the national press.

'I am from a religious newspaper
And we think our readers would like to hear,
If you had seen the kingdom of heaven
During your terrestrial journey out there?'

'I have seen closer the distant star,
Walked on the romantic moon,
Witnessed the earth from vast space afar
And seen all contained within a globe.

But no! I have not sighted heaven,
Near or many light years away
During my trip in the infinite beyond,
Nor picked up any indications about the way.'

'Oh dear! What shall we do
To alleviate the insecurity felt so,
To deal with the devastating shock,
The confusion it will bestow?'

'With sympathy that is in your care,
But this thought with you I will share;
The universe is such an infinite but minute complex,
We still know little of its revealing mix.

In your search to know the assuring joy,
Remember that truth anywhere may be found;
As say under a pebble on the shore
Lapped by the constant sea round.'

CANDLE GLOW

The candle shows the way,
Turning night into seeing day;
But the candle also wastes away,
Bringing the world to darkness again.

The candle creates the light,
Whereby we have illuminating sight;
But when it fades and peters out
The future will stumble all about.

It is sensible before the flame dies,
To use the glow to fire another flame,
And keep intact the vision for our eyes,
Maintain insight and espouse the wise.

Bless the candle bless the flame,
Bless the shine all intertwined;
Bless the action continuing the same,
Bless the candlestick maker by name.

Praise the father praise the son,
Praise the spirit three in one,
Praise those by whose hands,
The work on earth is ever done.

ESSENCE

Noise noise, one still small voice,
Rush rush, one right step enough;
Push push, degrading stuff
Top top, time to stop;
Light light, much too bright,
Collision collision, no vision.

Do not care do not care, who will dare,
Self esteem self esteem, yet all off beam;
Forgive forgive, let's live,
Unity unity, all in diversity;
Family family, like Trinity,
Old young, place in the sun.

Dawn dawn, do not mourn.

ST THOMAS

As a man of faith
Thomas comes down the list;
For his was no shining light
But of a dull pedestrian doubt.

A lack of belief in unworldly events,
And with no trust in his fellow men
To tell the truth and not fanciful things,
Was the hallmark of Didymus the twin.

Yet as a man in a world of pride,
He comes towering through;
Once proved to be in the wrong
He was big enough to offer no excuse.

A faith and lack of pride
Are two desirable needs of man;
Have been since anno Domini began
And both ideally should be hand in hand.

But alas!; how difficult it is to find
A golden coin with two faces so defined.

THE DAFFODIL

Blow soft your mellow horn,
And harmonise the day;
To the wind all tuneful sway,
And spring's reveille play.

Sprinkle the earth with yellow dust,
And reflect the glowing sun;
Herald the drab winter's past,
With the bright summer to come.

Stand tall on your wiry frame,
And carry the head with grace;
Show friendly a freshly washed face,
With colour the shade of youth.

Stir us with the flag of hope,
And raise those who will longer live,
You are the morning star on its way,
That fades after break of day.

More and so much more you give;
But still: your own private heart locked safe.

BREAK AND MAKE

To break is to destroy, to uncreate;
The devil's creativity, his genius
The strength and pulsating life drained,
The contour of beauty defaced.

To break in is to savage, to mutilate;
Roughen the tender internal sores,
Invade the inalienable privacies,
Leaving the dignity hurt and desolate.

To break out is to release, to liberate;
Unbind the strait-jacketed spirit,
To escape the gravitational restraint
Of this possessive Planet.

To break down is to understand, to solve
Man's understanding of Natural Laws;
The piecing together of misshapen edges,
The completion of the jigsaw puzzle.

To break is to multiply, to share,
God's largess, priceless yet free,
To all who knock, rich or poor,
At the one communion door.

YIELD

In a green land the reddest apples,
Are often at the top of the tree,
Beyond the reach of the picker.

They will fall in due time,
With the wind and the rain,
But will not store.

In a barren land the greenest desires,
Are in the soul of the sower,
Beyond the reach of his disposing.

His seed may grow in time,
Into the wind and the sun
But will not satisfy.

CHALLENGE

Near to Olympia it was once said,
Life is the race that before us is set;
Every New Year a further lap yet,
Each step a threading the marks of the past.

We strive to increase our running pace,
Keep ahead and break the tape;
But so do others in the race,
And competition becomes the driving force.

Let us resolve to share the prize,
The glory and the accolade,
With those whose talent falls too short,
Of that needed to enter the winning straight.

The calming of self, and the pure
Refining of the combative spirit;
Is I think the greater challenge true,
Than to podium stand with pounding heart.

Of the real race that St Paul meant;
Much more difficult to achieve in this event.

CONTINUOUS JOURNEY

On this perceived flat land,
Where people are sandwiched in a narrow band,
Between brown earth and a lighter heaven;
Is a far-off distant horizon.

A horizon where ground and sky meet,
And yet we know do not meet;
For the closer all try to get,
The same distance away is still set.

They also strive to know their maker,
Firmly shake hands at some spiritual border,
And for all that, still far away,
From the meeting for which they pray.

What advice then shall we give,
To those who wander as they live;
Awake under the misty clouds,
But sleeping through the bright stars.

It is simply this: to extend
The joy of the journey,
Not yearn for the end.

TO ROBERT BURNS

I have seen the cot where Robert Burns rocked,
One baby in his year amongst so many;
But why selected he to be the Bard,
Unless for a father's kindness and a gypsy's
blessing?

I have seen the banks from where he cared,
Lost the rose and gained the thorn;
But not for long for a man so born,
To turn a girl's heart in his youthful time.

I have walked the bridge over the Doon,
And heard the panting of Tom-O-Shanter,
Riding hard his galloping Maggie;
Pursued close by the host of the monster.

Long since did I these memories retain,
And I doubt they will be made again;
So old acquaintance never be forgot
Of this farming and relating to Scot.

From dust to dust his life spanned,
Rooted always in his native land.

ALTAR SHADOW

On the chapel altar a figure in its starkness,
Gilted and all aray,
By the side light luminous;
But the shadow beyond it see.

On the painted wall in its whiteness,
A replica of the story;
So plain, magnified, silhouetted in its darkness,
In the shadow before me.

Just the extended outline to witness,
No sculptor's impression given or suggestion
                                                    taken,
But open to liberated interpretation;
Through the shadow influencing me.

Of the figure in the calm stillness,
One more thing to enhance the fullness;
A reverse view now nears the completeness,
Caused by the shadow mirrored on the wall.

There ahead in its limpness,
All strength nearly drained away,
It now leads in increased lovingness;
As shown by the figure on the wall.

WILL IT ALL END WELL?

There is a light in the dark night,
There is a breeze in the stifling air
And a faith in the distracted life.

It will not mature quickly or easily
But with fits and starts gradually,
Nor with even hand or fairly.

Many have suffered and still will,
Not knowing where to lay their head
Whilst others sleep luxuriously in bed.

'Why does it have to be this way,
Does not the reality question the recurring day
Making it harder to steadfastly stand?'

There is little kindness in the self-centred world
And no hearing in the cacophony of sound,
For rampant man has now the upper hand.

But oh! An opportunist to the end;
He may well take over the promised land.

HEAVENLY SEED

O many bean seeds spread out on a tray,
Sorted and saved from last summer's decay;
What concentrated powder kegs you all are,
Each with the ember of life in your mottled core.

But first you must be lost to human eye,
And in a blanket of darkness lie;
Awaiting the firing spark to a glorious destiny,
Amidst an unlikely and earthy commonality.

This cycle of hibernation and life,
Must be protected with great care;
For insidious disease can take its toll,
Emaciating the continuing and evolving soul.

Not only you but your smaller kin too;
For the mustard seed is also so decreed
To act as a swelling leaven,
And produce a green and leafy heaven.

THE VILLAGE CHURCH

The rains have showered and drenched in varying
intensity,
The winds have blown and stormed apace in plenty,
Whilst the sun has beaten down in many a summer
fiery;
All the weather's changefulness throughout each
century.

And it still stands central to the village,
The hub of ancestral communal activity
During the reigns of monarchs and governing party;
Representing something not temporal, eternal to
each age.

The binding force it engendered maybe weakening
now,
The rims of its spoked wheel spinning apart;
But where we are is in no small way
Due to its standing at the village's heart.

Inside is no less humble and influencing,
For the walls are soaked in jewelled memory;
Latin chant by candle glowing, harvest homing,
Couples vowing, infants crying, families mourning.

The stone is truly spirit saturated
With human emotion from birth to death;
Forming the gateway where ghostly but real
                              pioneers have passed
And left their soul's essence encased and captive
                                         impressed.

Tradition and continuity are here to all who can
                                       imagine,
Pause and listen to the echoing wisdom given;
Not only in religious understanding,
But from a shrine to dignified living.

Who can say what another thousand years will
                                     bring
To village life with new thoughts striving;
But may an honouring and respecting solution
Be still the mode of any future evolution.

ANOTHER CASUALTY

The volunteer solider went to war,
A decent likeable young man,
Not for adventure not for glory;
But for country and duty.

His affectionate fiancée saw him go,
By nature a deeply serious girl,
Not for sympathy not for show;
But for God love and true.

They said very little,
Their tears told it all;
A taste of bitterness to the couple,
But hope and a promise in the eyes of the girl.

'Be quick and soon come home,
I'll be here when you return;
Then I will make for you
A heaven, yes, here in this town.'

The battles waged, the shells whined,
Comrades came and then sadly went;
But at last it ground down to the end,
The wave of destruction all spent.

The weary soldier left the foreign land,
A changed older young man,
By his journey to hell and beyond;
An affront to his idealism grand.

A time later the ring was returned,
Her love had faded and gone,
A budding bloom caught in a frosty bite;
Another casualty of a devasting strife.

SHADOW

Stub point of light,
Shining in heaven so bright;
Too painfully strong for normal sight,
So I turn away but still see
The shadow before me.

Stub point of heat,
Radiating through far distance great;
Too overwhelming for summer's day,
So I shelter under a leafy tree
But have the shadow before me.

Many sparkling faces of truth,
Aspiring quest of spiritual youth,
Difficult to comprehend and know;
But the passing over shadow
Helps indirectly to show.

Stub point in vast space,
Main source of all life;
Do not our loneliness compound
By fading away the shadow on the ground.
Sustain still our planet and race,
Prevent the earth's return to ice.

A RIVER SCENE

The Vikings came to Sandy
A long long time ago.
They brought fire and sword; took life cruelly,
A devastation filled with tears and woe.

The seas they crossed in narrow boats,
For this I give balanced praise,
They invaded this treasured land,
And here did strike a camp.

A river flowed near the site,
As it still does today;
A silver thread through the weave of time,
Having lost its stain of blood.

The ducks that eat my grandchildren's bread,
Now glide through this echoing scene,
With tall highly coloured prows
And red paddles leaving a two lined wake.

They are the reminder of an awesome character,
The sign of the Viking V;
And when together they take flight,
Oared by flapping wings,
They maraud the moody blue so vast,
Speared by the letter V.

REVEALED SELF

From the autobiography of my dreams,
There is one recurring story to relate;
Part of a deeper web,
Whilst on the surface the showy coloured pile.

Many times in troublesome sleeping,
The visions come strange to me;
Stressful and in a state of panic ending
Until waking brings a welcome reprieve.

I lose the familiar way,
I miss the bus I miss the train;
I cannot read the illuminated sign,
I take the wrong turning time and time again.

A taxi I cannot afford to pay,
So am stranded far from home
And the security there to enjoy;
Anguished by fear, cast away and alone.

What shall be made of this dungeoned thought?
The key lost under a forgotten stone;
Everyone has their own story to unravel,
But for me what does it have to tell?

Unless it is with humility to accept
That if on Abraham's journey of faith,
I would have been of such doubtful worth.

LOOK NOT FAR

A learned man can tell of many a thing;
Such as that our very bodily being
Is two thirds composed of water,
And cannot dramatically alter.

Another inspired teacher has revealingly spoken
With important and profound declaration;
That the Kingdom of aspiring heaven
Is very near and contained within us.

This time the proportion is not inlaid
For much depends on each individual case;
On how the response is made
To inwardly induced spiritual thought.

A small grain there certainly can be,
But a swelling can also occur;
If the nurturing is done with labouring care.

IN PRAISE OF ALDESTROP

Out of journeys that have no ends,
Only revised beginnings,
There can come, by chance or grand design
- who knows which -
An unscheduled, gradual
Or shuddering
Halt.

With impatient glance at our watch,
Petty malevolence in our heart,
We let down the carriage window
And thrust out;
Plunging into a pool
Of relief and ointmental soothness.

Oh! puzzling Lord,
Did You pull that communication cord?
For we have sensed heaven and its stars,
In a break, a short revealing break,
Then rumble, tumble on again
To other demands.

And all that can be done,
Is to rescue the moment,
From the waste bin of time.

For this, thank you Edward Thomas.

THE USE OF TALENTS

From each according to his ability,
To each according to his need;
A statement of truth to some,
An anathema to others of a different mind.

These are extremes of the playing field,
In the moving and living game
Where individuals can well shine,
But need a solid supporting team.

Needs are different to all who want,
In varying degrees so necessary;
For even ability must have its help
To develop that which endowment began.

Work and toil it is said will provide,
That required for all to thrive;
But when work is long and hard,
It is retrograde when it deteriorates to grind.

Work is often measured by success,
With no accolade if you fail;
Only one can win the set race,
Albeit more are needed for it to take place.

Count your blessings we are told,
Though first must acknowledge them as such;
Only then can we show compassion on those,
Who were in the shadow when God bestowed.

Why this should be so,
Is a mystery whose depths I find hard to know;
But I have no doubt,
That we should endeavour to modify it about.

The use of ability to forward this on,
Is a constructive role for any man;
The world in general may have a doubt,
But even its ways are slowly bringing change about.